SEOU

THE CITY

MW01096312

Lotte Depar

The 13-storey
and remains one of Seoul's most iconic malls,
partly due to its huge duty-free shopping area.
81 Namdaemun-ro, Jung-gu

Migliore

Another temple to commerce, Migliore's draw
is fading but its retail outlets are still popular.
115 Toegye-ro, Jung-gu

Cheongwadae

The presidential residence, known as the Blue
House, was finished in 1991 on a historic site.
Its roof is composed of about 150,000 tiles.
1 Cheongwadae-ro, Jongno-gu

Ferrum Tower

Designed by Korean architects Gansam, this
28-floor tower looks different from all angles.
19 Eulji-ro 5-gil, Jung-gu

Gyeongbokgung Palace

The first of the Joseon dynasty's grand palaces
has been ruined and restored several times.
See p027

Jongno Tower

Set on a major thoroughfare, Rafael Viñoly's
composite is more than the sum of its parts.
See p014

SK Tower

The 150m-tall SK Telecom headquarters was
devised by Hong Kong architects RAD and is
intended to resemble a giant handset.
65 Eulji-ro, Jung-gu

Bukhansan

Visible from almost anywhere in the city, this
three-peak mountain forms Seoul's northern
border and is a much-used national park.

INTRODUCTION
THE CHANGING FACE OF THE URBAN SCENE

Seoul is the epicentre of a colossal wave of Korean styles that have swept the world over the past two decades. It has become a leading supplier of high-tech gadgetry, and a seemingly unstoppable driver of popular culture, from K-pop to K-drama, K-fashion and K-beauty, all of which are having an influence on western mores. This once-drab destination has evolved into a global player. The question it faces today is: what do you do after you've well and truly arrived?

If current trends are anything to go by, the answer seems to be to keep on going. Its troubled past firmly behind it, the city is trading a relentless push for development for new, headier goals. The work ethic is now shared with a self-belief expressed in experimentation and a reinterpretation of tradition. Restaurants Kwonsooksoo (see p031), Poom (see p035) and Joo Ok (see p052) have won Michelin stars for their contemporary take on *hansik* cuisine. Reconditioned factories have been left raw to provide atmospheric backdrops for the burgeoning café culture. And the capital has become a shopping paradise, offering everything from hip streetwear labels to swanky beauty emporiums, while headline brands splash out on ever-more flashy architecture and installations to show off their flagships.

There are many possible bumps in the road ahead, not least economic headwinds, political upheaval and a bellicose neighbour to the north. But if there's one thing Seoul continues to demonstrate, it is the ability to thrive in even the most adverse circumstances.

ESSENTIAL INFO
FACTS, FIGURES AND USEFUL ADDRESSES

TOURIST OFFICE
KTO Building
40 Cheonggyecheon-ro
Jung-gu
T 729 9497
english.visitkorea.or.kr

TRANSPORT
Airport transfer to Seoul Station
The non-stop AREX takes about 45 minutes and costs KRW9,000
www.arex.or.kr
Metro
T 1577 1234
www.seoulmetro.co.kr
Taxis
International Taxi
T 1644 2255
www.intltaxi.co.kr

EMERGENCY SERVICES
Ambulance/Fire
T 119
Police
T 112
24-hour pharmacy
Jeil Grand Pharmacy
478 Gangnam-daero
Gangnam-gu
T 546 0093

EMBASSIES
British Embassy
24 Sejong-daero 19-gil
Jung-gu
T 3210 5500
www.gov.uk/world/south-korea
US Embassy
188 Sejong-daero
Jongno-gu
T 397 4114
kr.usembassy.gov

POSTAL SERVICES
Post office
21-1 Chungmuro 1-ga
Jung-gu
T 6450 1114
Shipping
DHL
5 Mallijae-ro 37-gil
Jung-gu
T 1588 0001

BOOKS
The Birth of Korean Cool by Euny Hong (Simon & Schuster)
The Vegetarian by Han Kang (Portobello Books)

WEBSITES
Art
www.leeum.org
www.seoulartfriend.com
Newspaper
www.koreaherald.com

EVENTS
Seoul Design Festival
seoul.designfestival.co.kr
Seoul Fashion Week
www.seoulfashionweek.org

COST OF LIVING
Taxi from Incheon International Airport to city centre
KRW60,000
Cappuccino
KRW5,000
Packet of cigarettes
KRW4,500
Daily newspaper
KRW2,000
Bottle of champagne
KRW120,000

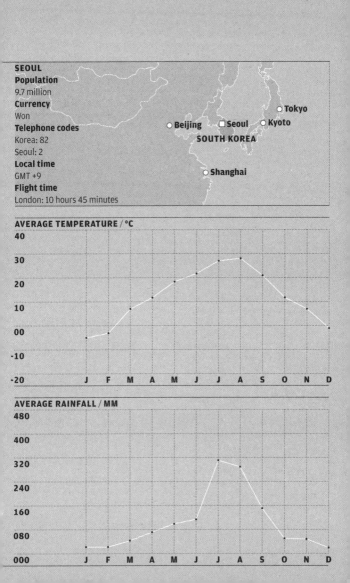

SEOUL
Population
9.7 million
Currency
Won
Telephone codes
Korea: 82
Seoul: 2
Local time
GMT +9
Flight time
London: 10 hours 45 minutes

Beijing

Seoul
SOUTH KOREA

Tokyo
Kyoto

Shanghai

AVERAGE TEMPERATURE / °C

40												
30												
20												
10												
00												
-10												
-20	J	F	M	A	M	J	J	A	S	O	N	D

AVERAGE RAINFALL / MM

480												
400												
320												
240												
160												
080												
000	J	F	M	A	M	J	J	A	S	O	N	D

NEIGHBOURHOODS

THE AREAS YOU NEED TO KNOW AND WHY

To help you navigate the city, we've chosen the most interesting districts (see below and the map inside the back cover) and colour-coded our featured venues, according to their location; those venues that are outside these areas are not coloured.

MYEONG-DONG

Financial firepower meets consumerism in this hectic hub. Big players roost here in a cluster of quirky buildings – from City Hall (see p009) to the distinctive Jongno Tower (see p014). Among these are the K-beauty brands, including Innisfree (see p080), and multiple gargantuan malls.

APGUJEONG-DONG

Art and luxury retail come together in an eclectic district home to shopping centres like Galleria (343 Apgujeong-ro, T 410 7114) and the infamous plastic-surgery clinics. But the real action is in the *meokja golmok* (backstreets), with their neon signage and designer-clad trendsetters. This is a great place to experience the spirit of K-culture.

SAMCHEONG-DONG

This leafy residential enclave fans out from Gyeongbokgung Palace (see p027), which is buffered by Bukchon's *hanok* buildings, one of the few remaining pre-war swathes. Its shops, upmarket galleries and *hansik* (Korean cuisine) bistros, such as Dooreyoo (see p046), have given it real cachet.

HONGDAE

Tucked away out west, this is as bohemian as South Korea gets, with low-cost housing, creative flair and an often boisterous vibe, due to the presence of Hongik University. There are vibrant busking and street-art scenes but also laidback spots like YRI Cafe (27 Wausan-ro 3-gil, Mapo-gu, T 323 7861).

ITAEWON-DONG

A predominantly expat quarter comprising embassies, US army barracks and English-language schools, Itaewon-dong is still the go-to 'foreigners' district. However, a band of 24-hour barbecue joints, gay clubs and lounges, and chic restaurants such as Parc (see p042), has emerged in recent years.

CHEONGDAM-DONG

Crowded with black BMWs waiting to pick up their affluent charges from Armani and Dior, this is the city's equivalent of Rodeo Drive. The high-rollers reside in the alleys behind western-style coffee chains. Seek out art venues like G Gallery (see p059) and dine on superlative Korean cuisine at Joo Ok (see p052), known for its vinegar.

SEONGDONG-GU

Once full of leather workshops and metal factories, this gentrified pocket is now, without irony, dubbed Seoul's Brooklyn. Instagrammers hang out in design shops and post-industrial-style cafés, including Onion (see p040), Zagmachi and Daelim Changgo Gallery Column (see p047).

SINSA-DONG

Bustling tree-lined boulevard Garosu-gil calls to mind Tokyo's Omotesando. Come here for fashion and streetwear brands like Low Classic (see p093) and Adererror (see p090), one of the capital's hippest labels. Find cosmetics at Tamburins (see p081) and relax at Cafe Mula (see p039).

LANDMARKS

THE SHAPE OF THE CITY SKYLINE

This massive capital extends across 25 *gu* (districts) – each divided into *dong* (neighbourhoods) – and is sliced horizontally in two by the Han river, which flows from east to west to the Yellow Sea at the North Korean border. Samcheong-dong encompasses many of the historical areas, including Bukchon *hanok* village and ancient Gyeongbokgung Palace (see p027). The unconventional Jongno Tower (see p014) serves as a gateway to the finance hub Myeong-dong, where you'll find City Hall (110 Sejong-daero, Jung-gu, T 735 8688), the stock exchanges and department stores. Commanding terrific vistas from the peak of one of the city's many hills, N Seoul Tower (see p011) is effectively the epicentre of the connurbation. Below it, bookmarked by Leeum art museum (see p028), Itaewon-dong might be where you spend much of your leisure time, as well as in Hongdae to the west and Seongdong-gu to the east.

On the other side of the river in the now-famous Gangnam-gu, life revolves around the sacred Cs: commerce and consumers. The streets of Apgujeong-dong and Sinsa-dong and the glitzy avenues of Cheongdam-dong cater to wealthy shoppers and socialites; the Lie Sang-bong HQ (see p075) and quirky I-Park Tower (see p015) jazz up their respective 'hoods. Just to the east of here, the soaring, majestic, impossible-to-dismiss Lotte World Tower (overleaf) has usurped all others as the poster child of Seoul's ultra-urbanity. *For full addresses, see Resources.*

Lotte World Tower

Architects KPF were inspired by the elegant contours of Korean pottery and calligraphy for the Lotte World Tower. It has a 'seam' that protrudes in the direction of the old city centre in homage to the evolution of Seoul. But it's the graceful taper that is its best design feature, ensuring that it does not overpower the surroundings, despite rising a neck-straining 555m. Inaugurated in 2017, with foundations stronger than those of the Burj Khalifa that can withstand up to nine on the Richter scale, it took only six years to build. Among the residents are a contemporary art museum and luxury hotel Signiel (T 3213 1000). In 60 seconds, the world's fastest elevator will whisk you to the 118th-floor viewing area, where the glass floor is just a frightening 3cm thick. *300 Olympic-ro, Songpa-gu, T 3213 5000, www.lwt.co.kr*

N Seoul Tower

Perched atop Mount Namsan, this 237m telecommunications tower is the capital's most conspicuous landmark. Designed by architect Jang Jong-ryul, it was completed in 1975 and opened to the public in 1980, and still transmits signals for South Korea's leading media broadcasters. Its uppermost section comprises two observation decks with panoramic views, as well as Korean eaterie Hancook (T 3455 9292) and, above it, the revolving French restaurant N Grill (T 3455 9297), which rotates 360 degrees every 48 minutes. A plaza hosts cultural events and exhibitions at the base. Private cars are banned from the area although the mast is accessible by taxi, and by cable car, which is the best way to arrive – the ride takes three minutes from the northwest base (83 Sopa-ro, Jung-gu).
105 Namsangongwon-gil, Yongsan-gu

Dongdaemun Design Plaza (DDP)
The undulating DDP is more amorphous
blob than conventional building. Conceived
by Zaha Hadid and inaugurated in 2014, it
stands in stark contrast to the drab malls
in the heart of the city's wholesale district.
The controversial complex, seen by some
as an expensive folly with little practical
purpose, comprises museums, shops and
cafés, and spaces that host major events,
such as Seoul Fashion Week. Yet, in reality,
there's not a whole lot to see inside, and its
labyrinthine interiors can be disorienting.
However, as a giant beacon (it is made up
of 45,000 aluminium panels), it cannot be
faulted. Visit by night to admire its backlit
facade, which projects displays that alter
with the seasons and reflects the shimmer
of the surrounding structures. Also check
out the Rose Garden, a field of 25,000 LED
flowers that illuminate the eastern flank.
*281 Eulji-ro, Jung-gu, T 2153 0408,
www.ddp.or.kr*

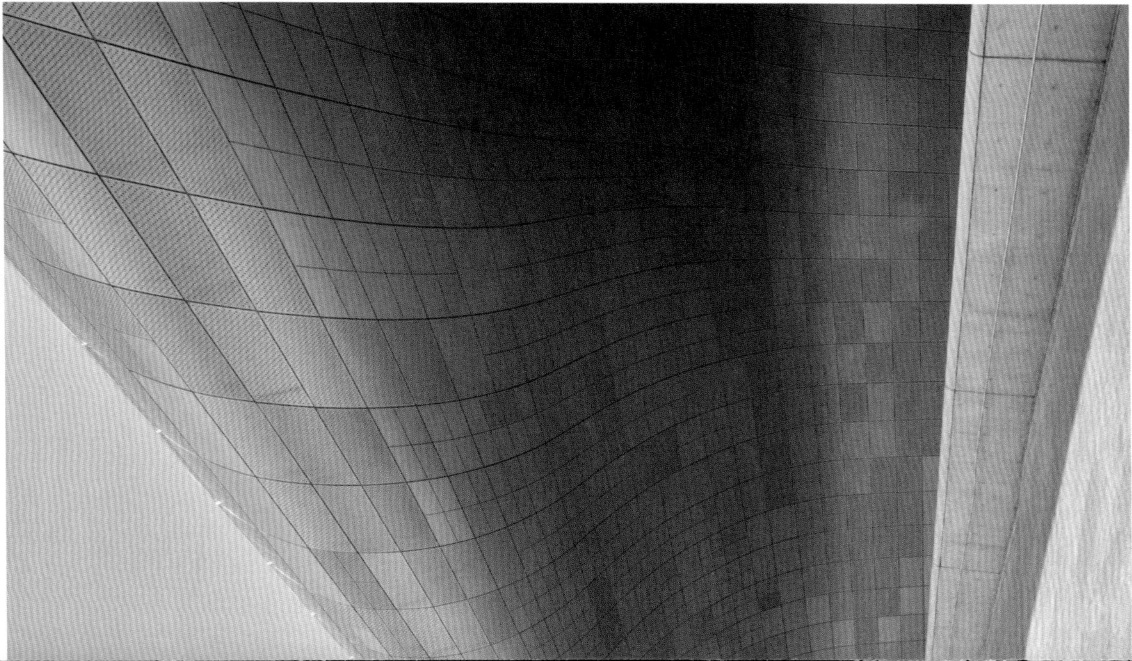

Jongno Tower

Unhappy with progress on its 20-storey tower, Samsung put a stop to construction and held a huge competition in 1994 in the hopes of saving the 17 storeys of concrete and steel already in place. Winners Rafael Viñoly Architects inherited the pre-existing form and overhauled the design, leading to a 33-storey mixed-use complex made up of three unique but linked volumes, opened in 1999. The 12-storey lowermost section has a convex glass curtain wall and above is an eight-storey flat-fronted rectangular space. High above these is the 'cloud', a double-height ring-shaped volume that is now home to a coworking space. To reach it, take the lift from one of the three cores at each corner of the roughly triangular frame. The 132m structure looms over one of the city's major east-west arteries.

51 Jongno, Jongno-gu

I-Park Tower

The former headquarters for the Hyundai Development Company was built in 2004 but got its bold facade by Daniel Libeskind and Himma Architecture Studio in 2005. Named The Tangent, the aluminium ring attached to the glass curtain wall is 62m in diameter and encompasses red and white geometric forms, and is reminiscent of the 1923 Kandinsky painting *Circles in a Circle*. It encloses various balconies and louvres.

A diagonal vector appears to penetrate the north-facing side of the 69m structure and protrude from its roof, creating a pivot of orientation for the area. The best vantage point from which to appreciate the artful exterior is the north-east entrance of the Starfield Coex Mall opposite. Also part of this complex, the 1987 KITA Trade Tower is still one of the tallest in the city at 228m.
160 Samseong-dong, Gangnam-gu

HOTELS

WHERE TO STAY AND WHICH ROOMS TO BOOK

Over the past decade Seoul's hospitality scene has received a much-needed boost. The bar for indulgence was set by the Banyan Tree Club & Spa (60 Jangchungdan-ro, Jung-gu, T 2250 8000) in 2010 as part of its transformation from banal mountainside bolthole to urban oasis. In the bustling centre, prime real estate can be difficult to come by but small homegrown brands and boutique hotels are finding corners to flourish: Ryse (see p020) and The Alcove (428 Bongeunsa-ro, Gangnam-gu, T 6230 8800), all stained wood and calm colours, and with a superlative rooftop bar, turned heads in 2018; Hotel 28 (see p023) proved gimmicks can be done tastefully; Glad Live (see p018) has taken a bite out of Gangnam-gu's nightlife scene; and Cappuccino (see p019) has its sights set on millennials.

The influx of such eye-catching competition has forced the old guard to seriously up their game: prestigious business address The Westin Chosun (106 Sogong-ro, Jung-gu, T 711 0500), constructed by the Japanese in 1914, was renovated in 2011, The Shilla (see p022) had a major overhaul two years later, and the Grand Hyatt (322 Sowol-ro, Yongsan-gu, T 797 1234) was spruced up in 2019.

Subdued, old-school glamour is encapsulated in the form of the Gyeongwonjae Ambassador Incheon (opposite) and Rakkojae (49-23 Gyedong-gil, Jongno-gu, T 742 3410), another *hanok*-style venue at which you can enjoy a slower pace in a more traditional setting. *For full addresses and room rates, see Resources.*

Gyeongwonjae Ambassador Incheon

One of the country's largest hotels to be built in the traditional vernacular, dating from the 14th century, the Gyeongwonjae was inaugurated in 2015. At the entrance, a two-storey pavilion and banquet hall in the Jushimpo style, which was developed in the Goryeo dynasty, is distinguished by an elaborate exposed ceiling, and provides a fittingly grand welcome. The 30 rooms, including two Royal Suites and 12 Deluxe Suites in their own *hanok*, are intended to evoke the serenity of Joseon-era culture, expressed through dark wooden furniture, *hanji* paper screens and rectangular baths, while also offering all mod-cons. For the most authentically Korean experience, opt for a *yo* (like a futon) and *ondol* (underfloor heating). Its location near the main airport is convenient if you have an early flight.

200 Technopark-ro, Incheon, T 32 729 1101

Glad Live

Opened in 2016 in a 20-storey steel-mesh-clad tower by Kim Sang-yoon, social hub Glad Live might be the city's most stylish artistic stopover. Its fourth-floor 24-hour lounge, with moss-green 'Mags' sofas and purple 'AAL 92' chairs from Hay, is in stark contrast to the scheme in the 210 rooms, which sport a cool monotone decor – the best come with herringbone floors and marble walls. Book the Live Pool or Glad Pool Suite (above) so that once the hotel's whisky bar has served its last you can invite fellow revellers back to a pad with a pool, a high-end sound system and a mammoth bed that can sleep (or not) multiple guests. More restrained but no less opulent, the Glad House Suite features contemporary art from the Daelim Museum (see p060). *223 Bongeunsa-ro, Gangnam-gu, T 6177 5000, www.glad-hotels.com*

Cappuccino Hotel

This hip 17-storey urban outpost is geared towards sustainably minded millennials. Its shared-value programme gives guests opportunities to donate to charity as part of their stay – in-room amenities that go unused, for example, are converted into donations or returned in the form of other benefits. The modern, minimal interiors by local designers Kidea echo the hotel's eco-friendly ethos. The 141 rooms have custom beds by South Korean specialists ACE – set on reclaimed wooden pallets in upcycling-themed Studio 1608 – and Ingo Maurer's playful light fittings made from recycled Campari bottles. The lobby, with its concrete walls lined with vintage clocks, is dotted with straw-filled seating (above) from Duwel's 'Country Chic' collection.

155 Bongeunsa-ro, Gangnam-gu,
T 2038 9500, www.hotelcappuccino.co.kr

Ryse

This 15-storey tower is as colourful as its surrounds. London-based Michaelis Boyd and local studio Integ designed the interiors to reflect the vibrancy of Hongdae, combining pink resin floors with Kenyan rugs and velvet curtains. The standouts of the 272 rooms are the five Artist Suites (pictured) by the likes of Laurent Segretier and Park Yeo-joo.
130 Yanghwa-ro, Mapo-gu, T 330 7700

The Shilla

Though it is the city's oldest top-end hotel and its name refers to an ancient kingdom, The Shilla is all about contemporary luxury. Opened at the bottom of Mount Namsan by Samsung founder Lee Byung-chul in 1979, the grand dame's 464 rooms, put together by Peter Remedios, feature king-size beds, marble bathrooms and yacht-style wooden bars built into the walls. West-facing units offer vistas of N Seoul Tower (see p011).

During the summer, the jet set gather at Urban Island, a third-floor oasis perched on the hillside with an outdoor and indoor pool (above) and Finnish sauna. Elsewhere you'll find Asia's first Guerlain spa (T 2230 1167), a retail arcade and five restaurants, including Ariake (see p044), set in a dining room exquisitely designed by Ueki Kanji. *249 Dongho-ro, Jung-gu, T 2233 3131, www.shilla.net*

Hotel 28

Opened in 2016 following the building's remodelling by local architects Dynagram, Hotel 28 is a swanky stopover dedicated to South Korean cinema. There is vintage camera equipment littering the hallways, and the 83 spacious rooms, co-designed with Australian interiors firm HBO+EMTB, are adorned with stills from the country's greatest movies, such as 1964's *The Red Scarf*. The Director's Suite (above), kitted out in collaboration with screen legend and hotel founder Shin Young-kyun, features furniture from Hermès, including Philippe Nigro tables, Enzo Mari chairs and a sofa by Antonio Citterio. There is even a museum of film history, as well as a rooftop garden, a library and a gym. The in-house eaterie, Wolhyang, is popular with Seoulites.
13 Myeongdong 7-gil, Jung-gu, T 774 2828, www.hotel28.co.kr

24 HOURS

SEE THE BEST OF THE CITY IN JUST ONE DAY

Taming this metropolis is a challenge. Most residents rely on the Naver app for assistance and we recommend you do the same. Our itinerary runs roughly north to south. Get around by taxi or on the subway – the circular green line 2 stops at all the major centres, including Hongdae in the west and Gangnam-gu in the east.

In Korea, breakfast usually consists of last night's leftovers so there is no 'scene' as such. However, Anthracite Coffee (opposite) can cater to westerners' morning whims. Nearby stationery store Object (13 Wausan-ro 35-gil, Mapo-gu, T 3144 7778), open at 11am, is worth a browse. You could spend the rest of the day soaking up culture at MMCA (see p026), Gyeongbokgung Palace (see p027) and Leeum (see p028). Alternatively, indulge in retail therapy at womenswear brand Mo Jain Song (257 Itaewon-ro, Yongsan-gu, T 797 6231) and multi-label emporium Beaker (241 Itaewon-ro, Yongsan-gu, T 070 4118 5216). Refuel at Seoul Coffee (see p038).

After dark, relax at Sulwhasoo Spa (see p030) before dinner at Kwonsooksoo (see p031) or try the Jinju-style eaterie Hamo (2F, 819 Eonju-ro, Gangnam-gu, T 515 4266), which serves *bibimbap* made with *yukhoe* (raw beef). Later on, Le Chamber (42 Dosan-daero 55-gil, Gangnam-gu, T 6337 2014), a high-end bar with a hidden entrance, and trippy cocktail lounge Alice Cheongdam (47 Dosan-daero 55-gil, Gangnam-gu, T 511 8420) stay open until 3am most evenings. *For full addresses, see Resources.*

10.00 Anthracite Coffee

Kick off your day with a drip coffee, a fresh scone and a huge helping of industrial chic. Launched in a former shoe factory in 2008, Anthracite now has five branches in Seoul. This one, in a quiet corner of Seogyo-dong, balances wooden furniture and floors with exposed brick and steel ceiling beams, and resembles a refurbished 1990s residential villa complete with a traditional garden. A hip crowd comes for the signature roasts, such as L'air et les Songes, a floral blend of Kenyan, Guatemalan and Ethiopian beans, and the unique flavours – the Butter Fat Trio mix conjures up roasted nuts and dark chocolate. For a further taste of local life, visit the nearby outdoor market Mangwon Sijang (T 355 3591) and sample street eats including *tteokbokki* (spicy rice cakes).
11 World Cup-ro 12-gil, Mapo-gu, T 322 7009, www.anthracitecoffee.com

11.30 MMCA

The venerable National Museum of Modern and Contemporary Art was established in 1969 and is spread across four locations throughout the country. The Seoul outpost opened in 2013 on a historically significant site. After the withdrawal of South Korea's Defense Security Command in 2006, the government tasked local architects Mpart with planning a museum that bridged old and new, turning the military building into the entrance and incorporating structures that were crucial to the Joseon dynasty for 600 years. The resulting cultural complex cleverly integrates exterior and interior spaces. Excellent exhibitions feature 20th-century luminaries such as abstract artist Kim Whan-ki, as well as leading lights of today's scene like Lee Bul and Suh Do-ho. *30 Samcheong-ro, Jongno-gu, T 3701 9500, www.mmca.go.kr*

14.00 Gyeongbokgung Palace

When founder of the newly installed Joseon dynasty, Lee Sung-gye, moved the capital from Kaesong in modern-day North Korea to Seoul, then known as Hanyang, he asked for a new palace. Construction began here in 1394. About 40 Confucian-style edifices comprised this compound but many were destroyed by Japanese forces in 1592. They were reconstructed in 1867. Geunjeongjeon Hall (above) is the largest building in the ensemble. It was from this grand throne, set on a double-tiered stone platform, that the new king conducted his affairs of state. Do not miss the changing of the guard at Gwanghwamun Gate – the palace's main portal has a double-roofed pavilion over three arched openings. The National Folk Museum (T 3704 3114) is also worth a look. *161 Sajik-ro, Jongno-gu, T 3700 3900, www.royalpalace.go.kr*

15.30 Leeum, Samsung Museum of Art
Opened in 2004, Leeum is split into three
buildings: for Museum 1 (pictured, left),
Mario Botta used terracotta tiles to reflect
the historic stoneware inside; Museum 2
(right) saw Jean Nouvel use glass to echo
the cutting-edge contemporary art within;
and Rem Koolhaas' black box houses the
Child Education & Culture Center (centre).
60-16 Itaewon-ro 55-gil, Yongsan-gu,
T 2014 6901, www.leeum.org

18.00 Sulwhasoo Spa

The flagship of homegrown beauty brand Sulwhasoo, which was founded in 1966 and is renowned for skincare, comprises spas, boutiques and lounges. Its original product, the famous 'Abc Ginseng Cream', is lauded in the first-floor Heritage Room. Elsewhere in the 2003 five-storey building, designed by local architects Iroje, are all manner of dedicated areas in which to test lotions and ask for advice. The holistic interiors by Chinese studio Neri&Hu are inspired by the symbolism of the traditional Asian lantern, evoked via a brass grid structure that runs from the entrance to the rooftop terrace. If you have time, opt for the 90-minute-long Intense Ginseng Journey, a luxury routine that includes a jade-applied facial, said to have restorative anti-ageing properties.
18 Dosan-daero 45-gil, Gangnam-gu,
T 541 9270, www.sulwhasoo.com

20.00 Kwonsooksoo

Celebrated chef Kwon Woo-joong has been turning out innovative contemporary fare at his two-Michelin-starred restaurant since 2005. He makes use of rare ingredients and house-made *jang* (a thick paste that forms the cornerstone of Korean cuisine) in the likes of *bibimbap* and *tteok-galbi* (short-rib beef patties) — all of which come mounted on a *dok-sang* (a traditional mini-table) and are presented in a variety of arresting ways.

We'd recommend the tasting menu, which might include *doenjang*-marinated chicken finished with a sherbet palate-cleanser and petits fours. Let sommelier Han Wook-tae walk you through the wine list. Winsome walnut furniture and dark walls feature in the refined interiors, and mosaic screens section off the private dining area.
37 Apgujeong-ro 80-gil, Gangnam-gu,
T 542 6268, www.kwonsooksoo.com

URBAN LIFE
CAFÉS, RESTAURANTS, BARS AND NIGHTCLUBS

Seoul's office culture and nine-to-nine shifts can make it seem strait-laced. But each neighbourhood has its own *meokja golmok* (alleys lined with bars and eateries) and locals approach leisure with the same dedication as they do work. In the past decade, the popularity of Korean food has exploded, and there are barbecue, *gimbap*, and spicy *ramyun* restaurants across the globe. Here, delve deeper to discover diverse offerings ranging from royal cuisine (see p035) to Buddhist vegetarianism, regional specialities like Andong *jjimdak* and Jeonju *bibimbap*, and hundreds of types of kimchi. Peruse the back streets for *tteokbokki* (rice and fish cakes in sweet chilli), late-night BBQ, *sul jibs* (alcohol bars) and pubs serving fried chicken.

While there are plenty of parlours like Neurin Maeul (7 Seocho-daero 73-gil, Seocho-gu, T 587 7720) that serve national spirits *soju* and *makgeolli* (milky rice wine), craft cocktails and wine are of the moment, delivered with aplomb at SAHM (5-6 Apgujeong-ro 46-gil, Gangnam-gu, T 070 4125 6413) and refined Vinga (6 Eonju-ro 168-gil, Gangnam-gu, T 516 1761) respectively, and Bonanza Coffee (24 Itaewon-ro 49-gil, Yongsan-gu) is emblematic of the international café culture. Highlights of the club scene are Soap (see p048) and Monkey Museum (B1, 8 Dosan-daero 57-gil, Gangnam-gu, T 541 9015). A night out is incomplete without a song, so head to karaoke joint Su Noraebang (37 Wausan-ro 21-gil, Mapo-gu, T 322 3111). *For full addresses, see Resources.*

Zero Complex

This third-floor Michelin-starred neo-bistro in the Piknic cultural complex was born of chef-owner Lee Choong-hu's passion for Gallic cuisine – he spent six years in Paris learning the art of French cooking before returning to Korea in 2013. Using seasonal ingredients picked from his greenhouse beside the restaurant, Lee treats diners to a new menu every few months. Past dishes have included squid-ink potato pasta and seabass bouillabaisse. This was one of the first venues in the city to champion natural wine – both here and at Bar Piknic below. Sommelier Clement Thomassin will gladly guide you through the list. Walnut '4110' chairs by Kai Kristiansen, 'Ghost' lamps by Shiro Kuramata and marble-topped tables from local studio Flat M all feature in the interiors designed by Lee's sister Da-eun. *30 Toegye-ro 6ga-gil, Jung-gu, T 532 0876*

Soseoul Hannam

South Korea's tough-to-define cuisine is untangled here by chef Eom Tae-cheol, whose fixed seven-course lunch and nine-course dinner menus change each season. He makes use of daily ingredients in dishes such as baby octopus with aubergine and pear, Jeju pork with miso mushrooms, and tender beef brisket with steamed abalone. The light, airy, monochrome interiors were designed to reflect the essence of Korean beauty without resorting to archetypal traditions. Areaplus worked with young local artists to fill the space with modern touches: walnut 'CH 002' chairs (above) by Craft Bro Company, ceramic pieces by Roh Gipp-eum and copper-and-tin installations by craftsman Kim Hyun-sung, which hang from skylights and resemble willow leaves. *B1, 21-18 Hannam-daero 20-gil, Yongsan-gu, T 797 5995*

Poom

Lofty in both location and its presentation of national cuisine, this Michelin-starred restaurant on the slopes of Mount Namsan opened in 2008. Designed by chef-owner and former food stylist Young Hee-roh, it has mahogany floors and majestic views. During the Joseon-era, upper-class families known as *banga* were sometimes invited to dine with royalty. Lauded recipes from these notable occasions were eventually passed down and became the bedrock of Korean gastronomy. Young offers a modern take on royal-court fare with local seasonal produce as part of a monthly menu. Past dishes include octopus in pine-nut mustard sauce, *sin sun ro*, a hot pot made with fish and mushrooms, and beef marinated in *deonjang* and dressed in soybean sauce.
*4F, 49 Duteopbawi-ro 60-gil, Yongsan-gu,
T 777 9007, www.poomseoul.com*

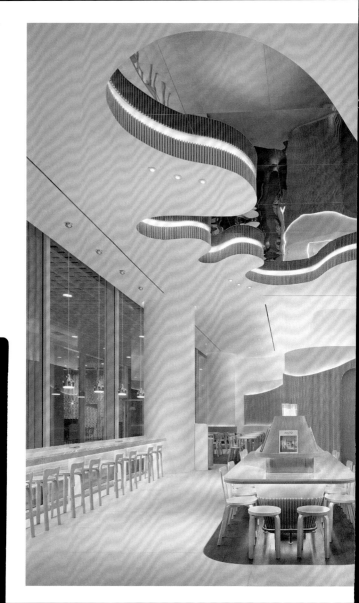

Cafe Aalto by Mealdo

Korea's lionisation of Nordic lifestyles and aesthetics has given rise to the ubiquitous Instagram-baiting interiors found in cafés throughout Seoul, as well as fashion fads, foodie trends and even companies such as Nordikhus, a locally based online platform set up to help citizens emigrate overseas. Designed by local studio Teoyang, Aalto is one of the city's first Finnish-themed cafés. Its birch-louvred interiors and mirrored light fixtures are inspired by the modernist oeuvre of Alvar Aalto. The ceiling cut-out recalls the shape of the architect's 'Savoy Vase', while his 'Stool K65', 'Chair 66' and '69' models provide seating. The eaterie is inside the Amorepacific HQ (see p078). Head here for a latte and fresh pastries conceived by bakery Mealdo. We highly recommend the Helsinki Pound Cake and the Honey Rusk, which fly off the shelves.
100 Hangang-daero, Yongsan-gu,
T 6462 5050

Seoul Coffee

When it opened in 2017, this became one of the first must-visit venues in the hastily gentrifying *hanok* village of Ikseon-dong. It was one of a whole series of new cafés and shops to retain an old-school facade but blend it with a minimal interior. Here, it was inspired by 1980s and 1990s Korean design (part of a more general revival of the era that was kickstarted by K-drama *Reply 1988*). Dreamed up by local studio Labotory, it has glass-brick walls and retro signage, and contemporary light fittings and brass-finished mirrors that provide contrast with the setting. On the counter are what appear to be bars of soap, but they're actually ice cream and should not be missed. Try the baked goods too – in particular the ang-butter red-bean buns.
33-3 Supyo-ro 28-gil, Jongno-gu,
T 333 0861, www.seoulcoffee.co.kr

Cafe Mula

This might be the café component of local athleisure brand Mulawear but its interiors are far from those you'd find in an average fitness venue. The place was remodelled by Korean studio Design5 in 2016, who turned a tucked-away old house into a permeable space bathed in sunlight thanks to its glass walls and roof. The airy oasis is full of softly curved furniture in muted natural colours, including Arne Jacobsen's 'Drop' chairs and custom suede sofas. Order a coffee and the famed 'king-size' green-tea tiramisu. Don't fret about the calories – Mulawear founder Jo Hyeon-soo holds yoga sessions here to help you burn them off. It is not that easy to find but use Exit 8 of Sinsa-dong station and keep your eyes peeled for its white-tiled facade, and you should have no issue.
13-12 Apgujeong-ro 4-gil, Gangnam-gu, T 6104 4541

Cafe Onion

The former metal factory now home to this fashionable café is not in a good state: its concrete floors are damaged, its brick walls are crumbling and its white tiles could do with a wipe down – but that's all part of the charm. The 1970s multistorey building has been allowed to retain many of its original fixtures but into this setting Korean design firm Fabrikr brought cushions to soften the edges and stainless-steel countertops that lend it a contemporary feel. The pastries and confections come courtesy of Bread 05 and include blueberry cream Danishes and excellent pandoro bread. The coffee is obviously the main draw but there are also seasonal drinks, which might include avocado milk. The industrial-chic aesthetic is highly popular with the Instagram army.
8 Achasan-ro 9-gil, Seongdong-gu,
T 1644 1941

Parc

Inspired by his own mother's hearty home-cooked fare, Pak Mo-gua launched Parc in 2013 with the intention of sharing her food with the world. His no-frills eaterie serves comforting dishes such as stir-fried glass noodles and spicy barbecued pork with rice and *banchan* (side dishes). Veggie plates, a rarity in meat-heavy Korean cuisine, are also available, and all have punchy organic flavours. The drinks menu features several varieties of *soju*, plum wine Maesil Wonju, and Baekwha Soobok, a rice wine similar to Japanese sake. Parc is inside a former residential villa, which enhances the cosy feel. The interiors are minimal and modern, with darkwood furniture set against white walls. The restaurant is located just a short walk from art haven Leeum (see p028).
26-5 Itaewon-ro 55-ga-gil, Yongsan-gu, T 792 2022, www.parcseoul.com

Juban

This bar-restaurant revolves around the hard stuff, dispensing spirits as old, if not older, than the surrounding Bukchon area. Try the 60-year-old Heobeok-sul, a rice liquor aged in oak barrels on Jeju island (see p099); Chuseong-ju, a 1,000-year-old spiced rice malt wine; and Solsong-ju, a pine-flower wine made in the valleys of Jirisan national park. Paired with these strong potions are dishes such as masala *jeonpyong*, an Indian take on the Korean pancake, and *saeng-seong* (fish) and soft potato purée served on squid-ink *lavash*. Chef Kim Tae-yoon's menu also includes *anju* (snacks) such as pork ribs. It is set in a converted *hanok* that still has its original beams. Kim's excellent follow-up Ithaca (T 542 7006) specialises in fusion cuisine. *12 Sajik-ro 9ga-gil, Jongno-gu, T 3210 3737, www.juban.modoo.at*

Ariake
With its smooth woodwork and clean lines, Ariake at The Shilla (see p022) is the epitome of serenity. This simplicity, deceptively hard to achieve, is equally evident in the cuisine – it is one of the city's best Japanese eateries. And while prices here can enter the stratosphere, they still represent value for money.
2F, The Shilla, 249 Dongho-ro, Jung-gu, T 2230 3356

Dooreyoo

After working in kitchens across the world, chef Tony Yoo returned to Seoul in 2016 to earn the 24 Seasons (T 772 9031) its first Michelin star. The following year, Yoo left and took over Doore – an old restaurant in Bukchon – added his name to the title and reopened it as Dooreyoo. The *hanjeongsik*, a multicourse meal formerly exclusive to aristocrats, comes complete with *banchan* including soy sauce that has been naturally fermented for seven years, several kinds of kimchi, and dried fish. Larger plates might feature deep-fried soy-marinated rockfish and steamed pork wrapped in zucchini leaf. It is surprisingly good value, making it an accessible entry point to high-end Korean cuisine. The establishment was granted its own well-deserved Michelin star in 2018. *65 Bukchon-ro, Jongno-gu, T 743 2468, www.dooreyoo.com*

Zagmachi

Opened by designers Studio ZGMC in 2014, Zagmachi is set in a former printing factory with a deceptively drab exterior. Inside the café, however, viridescent ferns, gardenias and succulents brighten things up, along with an assortment of furniture styles and hues. Many industrial elements have been retained to good effect, such as the vintage wood drawers used to display copies of the superbly put-together local magazine *B*.

There's a fine selection of drip coffees here, including the long black. But we say opt for the malty cereal latte, a contemporary take on the traditional drink *misugaru*, made of grain powder. Nearby, in a converted rice mill, you'll find hip Daelim Changgo Gallery Column (T 498 7474), a café and art space with walls showing off large-scale pieces.
88 Seongsui-ro, Seongdong-gu,
T 070 4409 7700

Soap

Designed by local DJ collective Pute Deluxe and Art Factory Corps, Soap is an intimate disco that can accommodate 300 people. Characterised by its patterned epoxy floor and curved interior walls, the subterranean venue features a lengthy undulating bar at which mixologists serve cocktails and the usual range of Korean and US beer. But it's the music that truly makes this place worth visiting. Soap plays nu-disco, hip-hop and house and hosts global talent alongside homegrown acts such as Lee Min-ju, also known as MushXXX, and Mellan, as well as live bands. It stays open until 5am and events start about 10pm; it's best to rock up around midnight. Also in Itaewon-dong is the semi-legendary underground dance club Cakeshop (T 010 7444 1926).

14-9 Bogwang-ro 60-gil, Yongsan-gu,
T 070 4457 6860, www.soapseoul.com

Mingles

This contemporary restaurant is all about mingling Korean, Japanese and European cuisine. Here, Kang Min-goo, former head chef of Nobu Bahamas, has been serving dishes like squid-ink capellini pasta with lobster, sea urchin and seaweed *jang*; and foie gras marinated in plum wine and then wrapped in kimchi, since 2014. His unique interpretations even extend to dessert, for which he creates sweets from savoury and spicy ingredients — ask for the *yumil-gwa* cakes, a deep-fried confection made from wheat flour, honey and oil. Since earning the first of its two Michelin stars in 2016, Mingles has become increasingly popular with international visitors, who clamour to sample the seven-course tasting menu, which changes according to the season.
2F, 19 Dosan-daero 67-gil, Gangnam-gu, T 515 7306, www.restaurant-mingles.com

Soigné

Local firm Studio Writers' interiors for this Michelin-starred restaurant are every bit as sultry as its name – which means 'well-groomed' in French – might suggest. The tables were custom-made, and partition walls finished with Nero Marquina marble divide two distinct areas: a 17-stool black counter (above) wrapped around the open kitchen, giving clear views of chef Lee Jun in action, and a 16-seat dining room with 'Armchair 33' chairs by Ton. Soigné serves a fusion of French, Italian, American and Korean flavours across fun (but certainly not frivolous) themed seasonal menus. For instance, Cuisine of the Three Coasts highlighted ingredients from the fishing regions in the East, West and South seas, including dried corvina barley risotto.
46 Banpo-daero 39-gil, Seocho-gu, T 3477 9386, www.soignerestaurantgroup.com

Joo Ok

Founded by former Nobu Miami chef Shin Chang-ho in 2016, this reservation-only Korean bistro serves sumptuous dishes as part of single set lunch and dinner menus, which change monthly. Past hits include deep-fried Jeju lobster with caviar, grilled rack of lamb with *chamnamul* chimichurri and, for dessert, chestnut ice cream with candied walnuts. Shin visits local markets and farms daily to source fresh seasonal ingredients. Any vegetables or herbs that go unused in the Michelin-starred cooking are pickled and later served as a *jangajji* platter. The venue has a simple achromatic interior – the primary decoration is Shin's sour house-made vinegar, displayed in jars on shelves, and proffered to stimulate the appetite. Ask for the *omija*-berry variety.
52-7 Seolleung-ro 148-gil, Gangnam-gu, T 518 9393, www.thejoook.modoo.at

Woorahman

Seoul's barbecue scene comprises Seocho Myeonok (T 489 1423), Myongwolgwan (T 450 4595) and many more. But our pick is Woorahman, which serves up premium Hanwoo beef (Korea's answer to Wagyu) in the likes of *doenjang-jjigae*, a soybean-paste stew with marbled cuts of tenderloin. The drinks list is the secret weapon here. Woorahman pairs malt whisky with each prime cut. As well as a wide selection of

classic favourites such as Ballantine's, the bartenders serve drams of lesser-known labels – try Lagavulin's peaty Islay Single Malt Scotch. Local design firm D:Plot took care of the decor, including the seven-seat granite bar and three private rooms, two of which are sectioned off by curved tinted-glass screens. Reservations are essential.
25 Sowol-ro 38-gil, Itaewon-dong,
T 797 8399

INSIDER'S GUIDE

CHOI JIN-WOO, FASHION DESIGNER

Together with his wife Koo Yeon-joo, fashion designer Choi Jin-woo runs womenswear label JKoo (www.studiojkoo.com). He is proud of his hometown. 'It's a fascinating city,' he says. 'Royal residences, temples and well-preserved historical dwellings are interspersed by skyscrapers.' He urges visitors not to miss the 'national treasures' of Gyeongbokgung Palace (see p027), Jongmyo Shrine (157 Jong-ro, Jongno-gu) and Bukchon (see p009), and to learn about history at the War Memorial (29 Itaewon-ro, Namyeong-dong, Yongsan-gu).

The capital's other great asset is its cuisine: 'Seoul is heaven for foodies,' Choi adds. At lunch he favours the namesake *samgyetang* (ginseng chicken soup) at Tosokchon Samgyetang (5 Jahamun-ro 5-gil, Jongno-gu, T 737 7444): 'You sit at low tables on a cushion on the floor – the Korean way.' And he might stop off for a caffeine fix at Cafe Onion (see p040). In the evening, his favourite restaurants are Redmoon (B1, 41-4 Hannam-daero 20-gil, Yongsan-gu, T 070 8865 3112), which serves Sichuan tapas, Choonsikdang (17 Dosan-daero 23-gil, Gangnam-gu, T 511 4022), where he often orders the *samgyeopsal* (grilled pork belly), Parc (see p042), for home cooking, and Daedo Sikdang (431 Hongik-dong, Seongdong-gu, T 02 2292 9772), a barbecue joint famous for its Hanwoo sirloin steak.

For an escape from the bustle, he takes to the cycling routes that run along the tributaries of the Han 'to enjoy the panoramic scenery'. *For full addresses, see Resources.*

ART AND DESIGN
GALLERIES, STUDIOS AND PUBLIC SPACES

In the 1960s, when the country's creativity was under the radar, the art world was stunned when Paik Nam-june exploded onto the scene with his Neo-Dada videos and shocking performance pieces. In the decades since, the contemporary movement continues to strengthen through groundbreaking luminaries such as Yi Hwankwon, who is known for his disproportionate sculptures, and Choi Jeong-moon, whose UV light-thread installations appear to be real-life wireframe models. South Korean design is having a moment too, as traditional skills such as bamboo craft are reinterpreted by leading lights like Kim Jin-sik (opposite), and Lee Kwang-ho (see p087), who combs the markets of Eulji-ro for unusual materials.

Alongside the rise of homegrown talents, exhibition spaces are growing in number and variety. Founded in 1970, Gallery Hyundai (14 Samcheong-ro, Jongno-gu, T 2287 3500) proved instrumental in launching the careers of many, including painter Chung Sang-hwa. Now there are hundreds of art venues in Seoul, from the bijou G Gallery (see p059) to the sprawling D Museum (see p060). Most are north of the river – for a handy snapshot, visit PKM (see p058), Kukje (see p070) and Leeahn (9 Jahamun-ro 12-gil, Jongno-gu, T 730 2243), established in 2013 by Ahn Hye-ryung, all in a cluster near Waryong Park. South of the Han, view public works around Songpa-gu and the sculptures in the Olympic Park (see p064). *For full addresses, see Resources.*

Studio Jinsik

Kim Jin-sik's sculptural creations, such as 'Shade' (above) – part wardrobe, part objet d'art – have a practical purpose. Inspired by *hanji* screens, he used woven bamboo to create a 'curtain' to cover artisan Kwon Won-deok's burnt-ash frame. It's finished in brass, the material at the centre of his Merge series, which also features a hotel bell and a door handle, all commissioned by the Korea Traditional Culture Center

(T 063 281 1500). He combined Tikal green marble and mirrored stainless steel in his Halfhalf collection of benches and tables, each piece a sharp yet functional contrast of geometries and materials. In 2016, Kim put together the installation *One Point*, a brilliant interpretation of a miniature golf course, for Wallpaper* Handmade. You can visit his studio by appointment.
www.studiojinsik.com

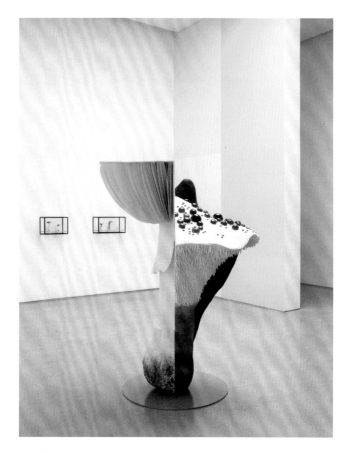

PKM Gallery

Founded by curator and Korean art-world veteran Park Kyung-mee in 2001, PKM has provided a platform for heavyweights such as photographer Lee Jung-jin, famed for her moody prints on mulberry paper, and Yun Hyong-keun, known for his imposing burnt-umber paintings. Abstract artist Bek Hyun-jin's oil-on-linen paintings appeared as part of 'Work Song: Soil, Mattress and Waves', which featured a weekly musical performance. Lee Won-woo's lighthearted exhibition 'How's the Weather Tomorrow?' comprised stainless-steel stars, clovers and hearts – all symbols of luck – as well as video works. PKM also presents global figures such as Olafur Eliasson and Carsten Höller, whose '50%' show included the resin sculpture *Giant Triple Mushroom* (above).
40 Samcheong-ro 7-gil, Jongno-gu,
T 734 9467, www.pkmgallery.com

G Gallery

Director Jinny Chung set out to dispel the often-intimidating gallery climate here. Her welcoming subterranean space has shown cartoonish works by LA pop art duo Shelby and Sandy and the whimsical scribblings of New York's Michael Scoggins. However, it's not all bright colours and comical themes, and there is a more serious agenda at play. Furniture artist Hwang Hyung-shin made zinc-plated and stainless-steel seating and tables for 'Layered' (above), an exhibition that explored the transformative nature of Seoul. Kim Sang-hoon's messy, misshapen sofas and bookcases, fashioned from high-density memory foam, were displayed in 'Foam Series'. Hanging woven-cable lights by Lee Kwang-ho (see p087), inspired by his mum's knitting, have featured too. *B1, 748 Samseong-ro, Gangnam-gu, T 790 4921, www.gexhibit.com*

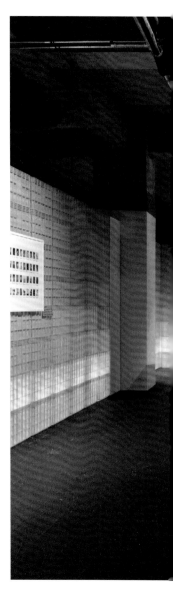

D Project Space

Daelim Cultural Foundation was formed in 1996 and now encompasses three distinct venues in Seoul. Its flagship, the Daelim Museum (T 720 0667), has become one of the most important creative strongholds in the capital. D Project Space was launched in 2012 and moved to its current location five years later. It is a champion of up-and-coming Koreans, such as illustrator Henn Kim and Rala Cho, whose film stills evoke oil paintings, and K-pop singer MY Q, who teamed up with director Kim Jong-seok in 'Mike' (right), which depicted the beauty of adolescence. D Museum (T 070 5097 0020) opened in 2016 to mark the 20th anniversary of the institution. Interaction is key here. Exhibitions like 'I Draw', which saw 16 artists show 350 illustrations and objects, are devised to foster engagement.
85 Dokseodang-ro, Yongsan-gu,
T 3785 0667, www.daelimmuseum.org

Arario Museum in Space

Elusive artist and billionaire owner of the Arario Corporation, Ci Kim (real name Kim Chang-il) bought this impressive building to display his 3,700-piece collection in 2013. Designed by Kim Swoo-geun in 1971, it was the headquarters of his architecture firm Space Group. He gave it a facade of black brick, clad in creeping ivy, to evoke local roof tiles and harmonise with the ancient Changdeokgung Palace nearby. Inside, the ceiling height increases floor by floor. On rotation up at the top, and in a vaulted basement, is Kim's treasure trove, amassed since he founded the gallery in Cheonan in 1989. As well as a hoard of Southeast Asian and Indian art, there is plenty of Korean interest. Seoulite Noh Sang-ho's 'The Great Chapbook II' (above) mined the internet.
83 Yulgok-ro, Jongno-gu, T 736 5700, www.arariomuseum.org

Choeunsook Gallery

Established by sisters and former fashion designers Cho Eun-sook and Sun-sook in 2008, this gallery/shop has an impressive 10,000-strong collection of ceramic, glass and wooden pieces produced by Korean makers. It has showcased the bronze and jade sculptures of Park Hyo-jeong and the abstract landscapes of Ko Young-il. Though it may cater to affluent, image-obsessed Apgujeong-dong, this isn't a venue afraid to challenge perceptions: Kim Chun-hwan, known for his intense large-scale collages made up of glossy fashion magazines, has had several solo exhibitions here. The 2018 show 'Art Life' (above) by Lee Se-yong saw works that recall *cheongwha baekja* (14th-century Joseon-era porcelain) presented alongside many other painted ceramics.
37 Apgujeong-ro 80-gil, Gangnam-gu, T 541 8484, www.choeunsookgallery.com

Olympic Park

Architect Kim Chung-up's 24m-high World
Peace Gate (pictured) ushers you into the
Olympic Park with cantilevered wings. Its
mural, *A Painting of Four Spirits*, is awash
with colours that signify the universe and
creativity, and depicts a dragon ascending
to heaven, which represents strength and
freedom. Within, there's contemporary art
at SOMA and a 200-piece sculpture park.
426 Olympic-ro, Songpa-gu, T 410 1114

Gana Art Hannam

One of the country's first major galleries, Gana Art Center (T 720 1020) was founded in 1983 and helped sow the seeds for South Korean art by championing such talents as oil-painter Sa Suk-won. Its second location opened in 2018 and is set in Sounds Urban Resort Hannam, a mixed-use complex run by lifestyle agency Kakao IX. Past exhibits include 'Weep Not', a showcase of pop art painter Eddie Kang's nostalgic characters, and 'Dialogue', which brought together the bright abstract paintings of Oh Su-fan. But the venue is by no means bound by typical white-cube presentation. Hur Shan's show 'Singularities in Daily Life' (*Broken Pillar*, above) blurred the lines between reality and illusion by creating a 'false' space of disorienting, out-of-place everyday items.
Unit 13, 35 Daesagwan-ro, Yongsan-gu, T 395 5005, www.ganaart.com

Orijeen

Seo Jeen's dynamic studio Orijeen created this chameleon-like cabinet as part of its two-piece Color Flow series. The plywood units change colour depending on your perspective. The wardrobe (above) cycles from lime-green to a medium blue and evokes the aurora borealis swirl, while a smaller sideboard flits between sky-blue and bubblegum-pink. The clever effect is achieved through a lenticular laminated surface made up of a translucent plastic sheet that is flat on one side and contains convex lenses on the other. The series is a precursor to Color Words, a 2016 project that saw two similarly hue-shifting shelves and a floor unit covered in the characters of the *hangul* (Korean alphabet), revealed as you move around them. Contact Orijeen to visit the studio and see them in person. *www.orijeen.com*

Gallery Yeh

A vital gallery in the country's art lineage, Yeh was established in 1978. Architects Unsangdong designed its current home, a grand tower with a concrete 'spatial-skin' facade (intended as a three-dimensional canvas) that looks as if it is folding. Within, Yeh unfurls across three modular floors in which local art sits alongside global, with works by Michael Craig-Martin sharing a space with those by Korean masters such as Paik Nam-june. Yi Hwan-kwon's clever sculptures, which look like skewed images and play with perspective, were presented in 'Encounter' (opposite). Yeh sponsors art throughout the city, including pieces by Ahn Sung-kyu and Cho Jung-wha. One of our favourites is *Vacation*, Yi's distorted reclining man near the World Cup Stadium. *18 Apgujeong-ro 12-gil, Gangnam-gu, T 542 5543, www.galleryyeh.com*

Kukje

A stalwart of the scene since 1982, Kukje now occupies a cluster of three venues. K3 (pictured) is the creation of Brooklyn architects Soil, who wrapped the building in a chainmail of half a million rings. It is committed to supporting Korean artists and has shown paintings by Ha Chong-hyun, portrait photography by Oh Hein-kuhn and installations by Yang Hae-gue. *54 Samcheong-ro, Jongno-gu, T 735 8449*

ARCHITOUR
A GUIDE TO SEOUL'S ICONIC BUILDINGS

Modern Seoul is vast, a snarl of looping roads, elevated highways and wide avenues, with little of the old city remaining. Concrete dominates, and perhaps the iconic view of the metropolis is of the 30 or so bridges over the Han. In recent years, however, an increased focus and willingness to experiment has added some compelling interventions. Among the most eye-catching are the Dongdaemun Design Plaza (see p012) and the Floating Islands (683 Olympic-daero, Seocho-gu), part of a drive to invigorate the waterway. Also significant is Leeum (see p028), a postmodernist cluster by Mario Botta, Jean Nouvel and Rem Koolhaas, whose varied treatments stand as a commentary on the fractured nature of the city.

Perhaps a lesser-known name is the late Kim Swoo-geun, the godfather of Korean modernism and founder of the Space Group, whose Kyungdong Church (see p079) is just a snapshot of a portfolio that numbers more than 200 buildings. Bridging the local obsessions of design and commerce is Rena Dumas' Maison Hermès (7 Dosan-daero 45-gil, Gangnam-gu), a double-glass cube of shimmering gilded strips at Dosan Park, and the Lie Sangbong HQ (see p075), another innovation in an exciting retail architecture scene that is fast rivalling that of Tokyo. Further afield, it is worth taking a day trip to the considered Paju Book City (see p103) for a glimpse of how things might look here were the concrete sheath to be lifted.

For full addresses, see Resources.

Ewha Womans University

Founded in 1886 as Korea's first modern school for women, Ewha is ranked among the best universities in the world. In 2003, the institution launched a contest for a new facility surrounded by the oldest edifices on campus. Opened in 2008, the winning entry by Dominique Perrault, whose work is distinguished by an almost absence of architecture (see Berlin's Velodrom and the Bibliothèque Nationale de France), sliced a valley into the topography – a stone-paved chasm gradually inclining down to a grand staircase that doubles as an amphitheatre. Inbetween, hive-like glass facades make a spectacle of academic life. Above, gardens conceal both volumes. By night, the void is illuminated by lights within the buildings, giving it the look of a giant installation.
52 Ewhayeodae-gil, Seodaemun-gu, www.ewha.ac.kr

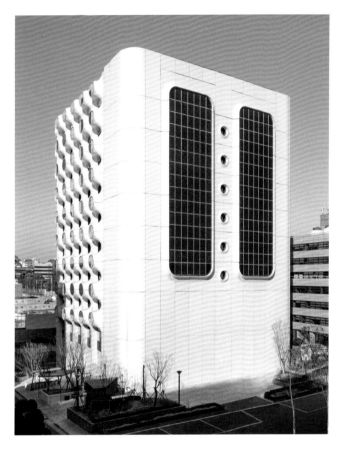

KEB Hana Bank Place 1

Formerly an unremarkable block for South Korea's largest banking group, Place 1 was reimagined by local firm The System Lab in 2017. Wraparound balconies were added to each floor, shielded by a secondary skin of 350 prefabricated modules of ultra-high-performance concrete with an undulating design that alternately recedes 50cm and bulges out 1m. The sucker-like protrusions hold 179 metal discs that spin in the wind,

perpetually altering its appearance. The inaugural discs featured artwork by names like Jin Dallae and Park Woo-hyuk, Kwon Oh-sang, and Lee Sang-won. As customers increasingly do their banking online, this is KEB Hana's attempt to revitalise its physical presence. It's open 24 hours a day and has a café, bookshop and exhibition spaces.
619 Bongeunsa-ro, Gangnam-gu,
www.kebhana.com

Lie Sangbong HQ

Sandwiched on a narrow plot between two nondescript buildings, this slim 2018 tower, a collaboration between Unsangdong (see p069) and fashion designer Lie Sang-bong, was intended to reflect his unique style and stand out among the foreign labels in the Cheongdam-dong district. The cloud-like curves of its front facade were inspired by painter An Gyeon's 15th-century dream-scene masterpiece. Made from ceramic panels, the vertical grilles are placed at varying intervals, adding to the sense of movement. Internally, fluted columns and arches evoke classical Greek architecture and contrast with views of the futuristic skyline. Besides a café and showrooms for the fashion house and Sang-bong's son's line Lie, it houses offices and residences. *451 Dosan-daero, Gangnam-gu, www.liesangbong.com*

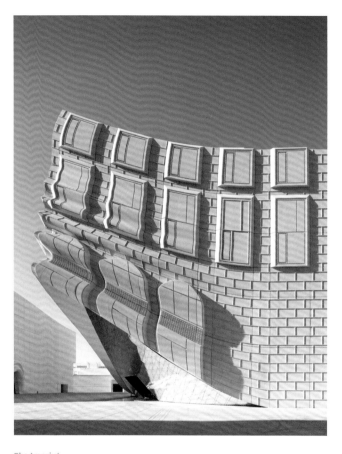

The Imprint

At Paradise City, an entertainment complex near Incheon airport, Dutch firm MVRDV was tasked with inserting and blending in two windowless structures to house a club and indoor theme park. Their solution for The Imprint, opened in 2018, was to design reliefs (or imprints) on each facade, made from thousands of glass-fibre-reinforced concrete panels painted white, that 'reflect' the nearby buildings. Wonderbox (above) curves to echo the casino behind it, and Chroma (opposite) is part-bathed in what seems to be a golden spotlight, which can be seen from incoming planes. An optical illusion makes it appear as if the entrances have been hoisted by a higher force, and digital-screen floors projecting visuals that bounce off mirrored ceilings entice you in.
186 Yeongjonghaeannam-ro 321beon-gil, Jung-gu, T 032 1833 8855, www.p-city.com

Amorepacific HQ

The country's largest beauty company has occupied this site near Yongsan Park since 1956. Its headquarters, designed by David Chipperfield and inspired by a 'moon jar' (a symbol of Korean beauty), opened in 2017. A seemingly simple volume, its brise-soleil aluminium 'fins' provide shade and give the cubic mass a sense of levity. A three-storey entrance atrium houses shops, restaurants and an auditorium, and is illuminated by skylights beneath a shallow pool of water, a defining feature of the central courtyard that begins at the fifth floor. Open to the sky, this vertical space maximises daylight and interacts with the city via three tree-filled terraces on multiple sides of the 23-storey building. The basement art museum shows off the late founder's collection.
100 Hangang-daero, Yongsan-gu,
T 4205 1757, www.apgroup.com

Kyungdong Presbyterian Church

Said to resemble a pair of hands in prayer, this 1981 house of worship was conceived by Kim Swoo-geun, who went on to design the Olympic Stadium (see p065). A scarcity of windows contributes to the fortress-like feel of the monumental red-brick facade, which is being slowly engulfed by creeping plants. The main entrance is found at the rear and reached via a sweeping flight of steps known as the Meditator's Walk – a literal ascent towards enlightenment. The chapel itself is stark and soaring – a silent, shadowy sanctuary that instils a sense of humility – with fair-faced concrete walls, cross beams, alcoves and wooden pews set at an inward angle to face the altar. Hung above is an enormous crucifix, divinely illuminated by a single 17m-high skylight. *204 Jangchungdan-ro, Jung-gu, T 2274 0161, www.kdchurch.or.kr*

SHOPS

THE BEST RETAIL THERAPY AND WHAT TO BUY

Perhaps the only thing that can match the locals' hunger for work and achievement is their pace of consumption. Department-store culture – spearheaded by the nation's various *chaebols* (family-run conglomerates) – is entrenched here. To sample it, visit old-money Shinsegae (63 Sogong-ro, Jung-gu, T 1588 1234) or the Lotte World Mall (300 Olympic-ro, Songpa-gu, T 3213 5000). Head to the retail hub of Myeong-dong to seek out top K-beauty brands such as the eco-conscious Innisfree (15 Myeongdong-gil, Jung-gu, T 776 0117), fast-fashion complex Noon Square (14 Myeongdong-gil, Jung-gu, T 3783 5005) and hybrids epitomised by Stylenanda's Pink Hotel (37-8 Myeongdong 8-gil, Jung-gu, T 752 4546) – six pastel-hued storeys packed with its apparel and 3CE cosmetics line. Many of the city's trends can be traced back to its textile wholesale district Dongdaemun Market (Cheonggyecheon-ro, Jung-gu), which is the perfect spot to pick up a *hanbok* (a traditional Korean dress).

For other souvenirs, try MMMG (see p094) and Zero Space (32 Huiujeong-ro 16-gil, Mapo-gu, T 322 7561), run by design studio Zero Per Zero – stationery is a Seoul speciality. You'll find ginseng, *soju* and tea (Osulloc is one of the best producers) in supermarkets but you'll want something to serve them in, so for kitchenware and celadon china, drop by Choeunsook (see p063), Sikijang (see p092) and Namdaemun Market (Namdaemunsijang 4-gil, Jung-gu). *For full addresses, see Resources.*

Tamburins

As with Gentle Monster (see p083) – also run by parent company IICombined – this is very much a brand to be seen with. Its signature 'Nude' hand creams, which are made with macadamia-seed oil, lavender, oregano and rosemary, are equipped with gold chains so that they can be toted about as if they were designer handbags. Other products include toners and serums that are equally appealing. Unlike many of the city's cosmetics shops, this flagship is no glorified pharmacy. The minimal interiors feature furniture by local and international artists. Look for the cheery wooden chairs by Luiz Philippe that have their front legs crossed and a stool by Yang Seung-jin that appears to be made out of balloons, part of the Seoul designer's 'Blowing' series.
44 Apgujeong-ro 10-gil, Gangnam-gu,
T 511 1246, www.tamburins.com

Rare Market

Founded in 2014 by Jessica Jung and Dami Kwon, this three-storey concept store has a futuristic feel – chrome accents, Perspex display pedestals, minimal furnishings – as well as playful elements. Clothes hang on a conveyor-belt-like system in one section and elsewhere on stylised gym equipment. Here you'll find unusual-for-Korea (hence the name) cult global brands like Regina Pyo, Marine Serre and Vinti Andrews, but seek out local talent such as menswear label The-sirius for complex tailoring in regular fabrics, and Blindness for sharp silhouettes and intense prints. In-house line We11done stands out for its eclectic, often unisex garments, including boxy cotton shirts in pastel hues, 1980s-leaning animal-print minis and offbeat jewellery.
24 Apgujeong-ro 80-gil, Gangnam-gu, T 512 3433, www.raremarket.com

Gentle Monster

When Kim Han-kook and Jay Oh's eyewear brand launched in 2011, Seoulites were seen sporting its shades all over the city. While many of its popular styles, like the 'Absente S1(2M)GD' in clear sand with gold temples, remain ubiquitous, the label has since diversified, and now features optical frames like the semi-rimless 'Blue Moon 01' in black acetate and gold. Don't forget the celebrity-designed limited-edition models; Tilda Swinton's 'Eye Eye' sunglasses in red acetate were a big hit. Gentle Monster has three gallery-like flagships in Seoul, which are renowned for their eccentric, out-there installations. For instance, the Sinsa-dong outpost hosted 'The White Crow' (above), a bespoke exhibition told over five floors using kinetic sculptures and art objects.
23 Apgujeong-ro 10-gil, Gangnam-gu,
T 070 5080 0196, www.gentlemonster.com

Vinyl & Plastic by Hyundai Card

Music Library (T 331 6300), an impressive archive of 10,000 rare records exclusively for Hyundai Card-holders, opened in 2015 in Itaewon-dong. A year later, the company took over the existing structure next door and launched an outlet for the public. Local architects Samuso Hyojadong retained the worn original facade but added an 8m-high glass-and-metal frame that encases it yet leaves it visible, and allows light to reach the interiors. Inside the two-floor store is a diverse collection of more than 4,000 vinyl LPs and 10,000 CDs, as well as other music paraphernalia – much of which is displayed on reclaimed pallets – multiple listening stations and a café. Storage, the basement exhibition space, shows a mix of contemporary art, film and design.
248 Itaewon-ro, Yongsan-gu, T 2014 7800, vinylandplastic.hyundaicard.com

87mm

This fashion house was founded in 2013 by three of the country's most popular male models: Kim Won-joong, Park Ji-woon and Seo Hong-seok – all born in 1987. Despite having no formal training, their inaugural collection of unisex streetwear launched online and sold out within days. The look has evolved into casual menswear with an urban edge – staples are relaxed-fit coats, cropped trousers, graphic tees and boiler suits with lapels – and 87mm's shows are a Seoul Fashion Week highlight. It set up shop in 2017 in a former residence, now all whitewashed brick with New Wave Street Culture painted on the driveway. The slick monochrome scheme reaffirms its motto: 'No concept, but good style'. Refuel at the café as you watch the K-pop world go by. *94-8 Eoulmadang-ro, Mapo-gu, T 338 1987, www.87mm.co.kr*

Kwangho Lee

Blurring the lines between art object and practical piece, industrial production and handicraft, artist-designer Lee Kwang-ho has been experimenting with enamel since 2009. He uses *chilbo*, a Korean technique that involves applying a glaze of crushed glass onto metal surfaces before they are baked in a kiln. This process dates back to the 15th century and gives his geometric copper pieces, which include chairs, tables and mugs (above), their raw, colourful look. However, Lee is not bound by traditional materials or methods. He works with steel and marble but also Styrofoam, nylon and, in the case of the works he created for the Yeonhui-dong branch of Anthracite Coffee (see p025) in 2018, Bakelite, a pulp-based plastic. Visit his studio by appointment.
1F, 12-6 Seongsuil-ro 1-gil, Seongdong-gu, www.kwangholee.com

Queenmama Market

Occupying architects BCHO's asymmetrical concrete box, which has a part-cantilevered cedar shed perched on top, Queenmama Market is an unexpectedly lush plant-filled oasis in the centre of Gangnam-gu. Opened in 2015 by Kang Jin-young and Yoon Hanni, from whose nickname the concept store takes its name, it offers a rotating selection of unusual and everyday objects sourced from around the world. From ceramics and sponges to musical instruments and tools, and cosmetics by the likes of Tamburins (see p081), the shopping here has an air of spontaneity. There's also a level totally dedicated to books. Manufact Coffee's top-floor outdoor terrace is a fine eyrie from which to enjoy a cold brew and panoramic views of the upmarket neighbourhood. *50 Apgujeong-ro 46-gil, Gangnam-gu, T 070 4281 3372, www.queenmamamarket.com*

Print Bakery

South Korea's oldest bidding house, Seoul Auction, opened Print Bakery in 2012. True to its name, the multistorey gallery/shop, designed by local studio Gute Form, sells a large range of limited-edition art prints, including those by contemporary Korean talents such as Chang Uc-chin and Park Seo-bo. Lifestyle products like Ku Min-sun's paint-splattered ceramic coffee cups, bags emblazoned with works by Choi Kyung-joo, and Son Jung-min's cheerful umbrellas are on sale too. The store also hosts talks featuring Seoul creatives, and exhibitions. Moonj's stylish monochrome illustrations were displayed as part of the 2018 show 'Stranger in Town', which encompassed *Kyoto* (above, left) and *Hoian* (right), as well as larger pieces on hung fabric.
*87 Dokseodang-ro, Yongsan-gu,
T 795 5888, www.printbakery.com*

Adererror

One of South Korea's most dynamic street brands, Adererror is also one of its most anonymous – its founders are deliberately elusive. Launching in 2014 with skater-style hoodies, tees and caps, its collections now include tailored trousers, knitwear, shirts, jackets and overcoats. What all the pieces have in common is a 'futro' (future-retro) vibe and a voluminous outline that suits the unisex stance. The label is worshipped on social media, and the seasonal installations in its flagship are like catnip to influencers. Think flower-filled urinals, neon signs, piles of old-school computers and art created in collaboration with influential galleries such as D Project Space (see p060). Look out for soap embossed with cheeky slogans from spin-off lifestyle line Day After Day.
19-18 Wausan-ro 21-gil, Mapo-gu,
T 3143 2221, www.adererror.com

Sikijang

The title of Chung So-yeong's studio refers to both a person who makes tableware and a cupboard in which it can be stored. Chung started the enterprise in 2005 to specialise in the kind of clean-lined, sleek items that are typical of Korean craft — tablemats with an *ottchil* (natural lacquer) finish, fine glass bowls and perfectly imperfect porcelain. Cutlery is also a major facet of the Sikijang repertoire. As well as shapely copper-and- silver dessert spoons, the emporium sells sets such as Kim Il-woong's chopsticks and spoon (above, KRW65,000), made of *yugi*, a copper-tin alloy with a sterilising effect. Exhibitions are held here in collaboration with Gallery Wannmul (T 3446 6480), and showcase the likes of Kang Jun-su's leather bowls and Cho Hyun-sung's goblets.
751 Samseong-ro, Gangnam-gu,
T 541 6480, www.sikijang.com

Low Classic

Lee Myung-sin, Hwang Hyng-ji and Park Jin-seon's label has been heralded as the Phoebe Philo-era Celine of South Korea, known for its loosely tailored silhouettes with unusual twists, and upscale fabrics. There are checked cotton skirts with over-scaled pleats, generously sized double-breasted wool blazers and leather bags in slightly off-kilter shapes. The interior of the multistorey shop features natural materials combined with punchy accents such as concrete walls, grey-brick floors, orange Perspex shelving and multi-hued marble plinths, arranged in clusters. Its more youthful, street-oriented diffusion line Locle encompasses puffers in lilac and other pastels, velvet sweatpants and preppy caps emblazoned with logos. *57 Nonhyeon-ro 159-gil, Gangnam-gu, T 516 2004, www.lowclassic.com*

Millimeter Milligram

The South Korean capital has no shortage of consummate stationery shops but this might be its greatest. Millimeter Milligram (MMMG) sells the kind of cheery minutiae that Seoul does so well and is an ideal place to source gifts for the hard-to-please. The products here range from colourful totes, tea towels and notepads to greetings cards and leather pouches and pencil cases, all designed in-house. You'll even find clothing accessories: the two-tone 'Muffler' scarves are 100 per cent wool and knitted by local maker Misu A Barbe. MMMG began in 1999 as a design studio and has since opened a further two stores across the city. It is also the country's first wholesaler for hip Swiss label Freitag, known for its resilient bags created using recycled truck tarpaulins.
240 Itaewon-ro, Yongsan-gu, T 549 1520, www.mmmg.net

Boon the Shop

Since the millennium, this vast fashion-and-lifestyle enterprise has positioned itself as the city's headline seller of global names, from Tom Ford to The Row. It also promotes homegrown labels including Refur, I Hate Monday, Portrait Report, Xte and Suel, as well as its namesake line, which majors in high-end suiting and reversible outerwear. The seven-storey flagship was designed by Peter Marino – two angular volumes clad in white marble, split into youth and classic retail inside, are linked by a glass bridge. Interiors feature bare concrete walls and mirrored stainless steel, and incorporate a café and rooftop restaurant. Its sister (or brother) brand Boon on the Moon resides in department stores across the country, proffering edgy menswear and boys' toys. *21 Apgujeong-ro 60-Gil, Gangnam-gu, T 2056 1234, www.boontheshop.com*

ESCAPES

WHERE TO GO IF YOU WANT TO LEAVE TOWN

The dramatic natural environment surrounding the capital offers respite from the urban grind. Popular escapes near Seoul are the lush Oak Valley (opposite) and the ski resort of Yongpyong (see p102) near Gangneung, from where you can catch a ferry to the wonderfully undiscovered Ulleung island and stay at the futuristic Kosmos Hotel (see p100). Far more developed, Jeju island, located south of the peninsula, is an hour by plane or overnight by boat. This subtropical volcanic outcrop is dominated by 1,950m Mount Hallasan, the tallest peak in the country, and the national park, with its lava caves and craters, contains rare plant and animal species. The Museum of Art (see p099) is indicative of Jeju's ambitions to transcend the surf-and-sand offerings of the region's other beach resorts. From here, catch a ferry to the southernmost spot in Korea, Marado, which is known for its marine life, to stay with one of its 100 residents in a *minbak* (B&B) for a glimpse of a rural way of life.

The high-speed KTX rail link has brought South Korea's second-largest city, Busan, within easy reach – trains take two-and-a-half hours to reach this once rough-and-tumble port. Still gritty in places, it has blossomed into one of Asia's film epicentres; a star-studded annual festival is staged in the Coop Himmelblau-designed Busan Cinema Center (1467 U1-dong, Haeundae-gu, T 051 780 6000), an imposing, wing-shaped structure in gentrified Haeundae Beach. *For full addresses, see Resources.*

Museum SAN, Oak Valley, Wonju-si

Nestled in the Wonju mountains, Museum SAN is dedicated to the interaction of art and nature, and circulation is guided via a series of structures strung 700m along the hillside. A path winds through the flower garden past Mark di Suvero's red steel *For Gerard Manley Hopkins* (above) and under Alexander Liberman's *Archway* by a water feature to the main building, designed by Tadao Ando. Four concrete boxes clad in paju stone and connected via courtyards house the Paper Gallery, dedicated to the Korean craft, and the Cheongjo Gallery, showcasing regional contemporary works. Pass through the stone sculpture garden, where mounds evoke Silla tombs, to the four works in the James Turrell exhibition hall. It is a 90-minute drive from Seoul. *260 Okeubaelli 2-gil, Gangwon-do, T 033 730 9000, www.museumsan.org*

Anyang Pavilion, Anyang-si

In 2005, Portuguese legend Álvaro Siza Vieira was asked to create a structure for the entrance to the Art Park in Anyang, a satellite suburb 20km south of Seoul and home of the ambitious Anyang Public Art Project. He accepted the commission and was then joined by long-time collaborator Carlos Castanheira and Korean architect Kim Jun-sung, masterplanner of Heyri Art Valley. The final design – a gently curved pavilion – typifies Siza Vieira's minimalist approach. Its shell is made from a concrete so fine it's almost white, and large windows flood the interiors with light. It opened in 2006, earning him a local following – the same team went on to devise the Mimesis Art Museum, an undulating mass opened in 2010, in Paju Book City (see p103).

Anyang 2(i)-dong, Manan-gu, Gyeonggi-do, T 031 687 0548, www.ayac.or.kr

Jeju Museum of Art, Jeju-do

Seoul architects Gansam's ethereal, almost haunting building, realised in concrete and stone and framed by giant colonnades on two sides, is a network of indoor/outdoor display areas. It is a monumental structure yet, surrounded by a pool in which it seems to float, it blends easily into its beautiful setting in the foothills of Hallasan National Park (see p096). Equally impressive is the collection shown inside, which mines the island's under-celebrated tradition. Works are often nature-inspired, for instance the oeuvre of veteran painter Chang Ree-suok, housed here in its entirety. There are also temporary exhibitions, such as large-scale hi-tech installations by Kimchi and Chips, and Kim Soo Nam's photo documentary of national folk culture and shamanic rituals. *2894-78, 1100-ro, Jeju-si, T 064 710 4300, jmoa.jeju.go.kr*

Kosmos, Ulleung-do

This unspoilt volcanic island in the Sea of Japan is a place of jagged peaks, odd rock formations, caves, cedar forests, pebble beaches and rugged coast. Perched on a cliff, this hotel is housed in a pair of white concrete organic structures with seashell-like interiors, sculpted by The System Lab (see p074). Villa Kosmos sleeps up to eight in dramatic high-ceilinged spaces (above) that spiral out from a courtyard with an indoor pool and a jacuzzi on the terrace; there are double and *ondol* rooms in the other wing. Ex-Noma chef Hwang Sun-jin does wonders with local ingredients – try the *honghapbap* (mussels on rice). To get here is quite an undertaking – two-and-a-half hours on the train to Gangneung and then an often choppy three-hour ferry ride. *88-13 Chusan-gil, Buk-myeon, T 054 791 7788, www.thekosmos.co.kr*

Yongpyong Resort, Gangwon-do

Opened at the foot of Balwangsan in 1975, this winter paradise two and a half hours' drive from the capital is at the forefront of South Korea's fast developing ski industry. Also known as Dragon Valley, it often hosts international competitions, most notably the slalom at the 2018 Olympics, although there are also novice-friendly slopes, and the gondola up to the peak offers a super view of the demilitarised zone 80km away.

The season runs from mid-November until early April. To escape the hoi polloi, book a suite in the hanok-style Korea Palace hotel (T 033 336 1111), modelled on a traditional Goryeo-era building, which is 15 minutes out of town by car. The deep sunken wood baths provide heavenly off-piste recovery. *130 Yongsan-ri, Daegwallyeong-myeon, Pyeongchang-gun, T 033 335 5757, www.yongpyong.co.kr*

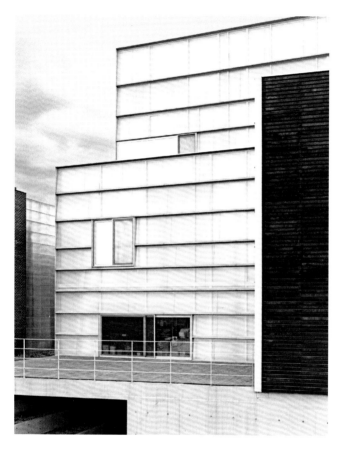

Paju Book City, Paju-si

An hour north of Seoul are two innovative communities – Paju Book City, the centre of South Korea's publishing industry, and Heyri Art Valley, originally built to house its workers. The latter has since evolved into a haphazard colony of craftspeople, writers, architects, filmmakers, musicians and painters. The stringent architectural guidelines require that all the buildings, from homes in sculpted concrete to the partly black-steel-covered Youlhwadang Publishers (above), use materials such as polycarbonate, copper, plywood and glass, which meld with the colours and contours of the landscape. This commitment lends harmony to the development and allows it to blend with its environment, making for an impressive but unobtrusive complex.
145 Hoedong-gil, Gyeonggi-do,
T 031 995 0050, www.pajubookcity.org

NOTES
SKETCHES AND MEMOS

RESOURCES
CITY GUIDE DIRECTORY

HOTELS
ADDRESSES AND ROOM RATES

The Alcove 016
Room rates:
double, from KRW90,000
428 Bongeunsa-ro
Gangnam-gu
T 6230 8800
www.accorhotels.com

Banyan Tree Club & Spa 016
Room rates:
double, from KRW340,000
60 Jangchungdan-ro
Jung-gu
T 2250 8000
www.banyantree.com

Cappuccino Hotel 019
Room rates:
double, from KRW110,000;
Studio 1608, from KRW320,000
155 Bongeunsa-ro
Gangnam-gu
T 2038 9500
www.hotelcappuccino.co.kr

Glad Live 018
Room rates:
double, from KRW110,000;
Glad House Suite, from KRW500,000;
Live Pool Suite, from KRW1,500,000;
Glad Pool Suite, from KRW1,500,000
223 Bongeunsa-ro
Gangnam-gu
T 6177 5000
www.glad-hotels.com

Grand Hyatt Seoul 016
Room rates:
double, from KRW250,000
322 Sowol-ro
Yongsan-gu
T 797 1234
www.hyatt.com

Gyeongwonjae Ambassador Incheon 017
Room rates:
double, from KRW250,000;
Deluxe Suite, from KRW400,000;
Royal Suite, from KRW650,000
200 Technopark-ro
Incheon
T 032 729 1101
www.accorhotels.com

Korea Palace 102
Room rates:
double, from KRW200,000
1169 Olympic-ro
Daegwallyeong-myeon
Pyeongchang-gun
Gangwon-do
T 033 336 1111
www.koreapalace.co.kr

Kosmos 100
Room rates:
double, from KRW350,000;
Ondol, from KRW390,000;
Villa Kosmos, from KRW10,000,000
88-13 Chusan-gil
Buk-myeon
Ulleung-do
T 054 791 7788
www.thekosmos.co.kr

Rakkojae 016
Room rates:
double, from KRW230,000
49-23 Gyedong-gil
Jongno-gu
T 742 3410
www.rkj.co.kr

Ryse 020
Room rates:
double, from KRW220,000;
Artist Suite, from KRW800,000
130 Yanghwa-ro
Mapo-gu
T 330 7700
www.rysehotel.com

The Shilla 022
Room rates:
double, from KRW355,000
249 Dongho-ro
Jung-gu
T 2233 3131
www.shilla.net

Signiel 010
Room rates:
double, from KRW342,000
76-101F
Lotte World Tower
300 Olympic-ro
Songpa-gu
T 3213 1000
www.lottehotel.com/seoul-signiel

Hotel 28 023
Room rates:
double, from KRW220,000;
The Director's Suite, from KRW1,100,000
13 Myeongdong 7-gil
Jung-gu
T 774 2828
www.hotel28.co.kr

The Westin Chosun 016
Room rates:
double, from KRW210,000
106 Sogong-ro
Jung-gu
T 711 0500
www.marriott.com

WALLPAPER* CITY GUIDES

Executive Editor
Jeremy Case

Author
Crystal Tai

Photography Editor
Rebecca Moldenhauer

Art Editor
Jade R Arroyo

Senior Sub-Editor
Sean McGeady

Editorial Assistant
Josh Lee

Contributors
Hahyun Joo
Katarzyna Puchowska
Rachel Ward
Olivia Berry
Belle Place
George Greenhill
Fiona Bae
Karryn Miller
Rhiannon Shepherd
Jonathan Hopfner

Intern
Alex Merola

Seoul Imprint
First published 2008
Third edition 2019

ISBN 978 0 7148 7902 4

More City Guides
www.phaidon.com/travel

Follow us
@wallpaperguides

Contact
wcg@phaidon.com

Original Design
Loran Stosskopf

Map Illustrator
Russell Bell

Production Controller
Gif Jittiwutikarn

Assistant Production Controller
Lily Rodgers

Wallpaper* Magazine
161 Marsh Wall
London E14 9AP
contact@wallpaper.com

Wallpaper*® is a registered trademark of TI Media

Phaidon Press Limited
Regent's Wharf
All Saints Street
London N1 9PA

Phaidon Press Inc
65 Bleecker Street
New York, NY 10012

All prices and venue information are correct at time of going to press, but are subject to change.

A CIP Catalogue record for this book is available from the British Library.

PHOTOGRAPHERS

Choi Yong-joon
Seoul city view,
inside front cover
Lotte World Tower, p010
Dongdaemun Design
Plaza, pp012-013
Glad Live, p018
Hotel 28, p023
Anthracite Coffee, p025
MMCA, p026
Gyeongbokgung
Palace, p027
Kwonsooksoo, p031
Zero Complex, p033
Soseoul Hannam, p034
Seoul Coffee, p038
Cafe Mula, p039
Cafe Onion, pp040-041
Parc, p042
Juban, 043
Dooreyoo, p046
Soap, p048
Mingles, p049
Soigné, pp050-051
Joo OK, p052
Woorahman, p053
G Gallery, p059
D Project Space,
pp060-061
Arario Museum in
Space, p062
Choeunsook Gallery, p063
Gallery Yeh, p068
Ewha Women's
University, p073

KEB Hana Bank
Place 1, p074
Tamburins, p081
Rare Market, p082
87mm, p086
Queenmama Market, p088
Print Bakery, p089
Adererror, p090, p091
Low Classic, p093
Millimeter Milligram, p094
Boon the Shop, p095

Andrea Buso
Capuccino Hotel, p019

Tim Franco
Choi Jin-woo, p055

Marc Gerritsen
Jongno Tower, p014
Kyungdong Presbyterian
Church, p079

Fernando Guerra
Anyang Pavilion, p098

Chin Hyo-sook
Vinyl & Plastic by Hyundai
Card, pp084-085

Kim Jae-yun
Lie Sangbong HQ, p075

Kim Yong-kwan
Kukje Gallery, pp070-071
Kosmos, p100, p101

Isaac Maiselman
Ryse, pp020-021

Mulnamoo
Studio Jinsik, p057

MVRDV
The Imprint, p076, p077

Noshe
Amorepacific HQ, p078

Shin Kyung-sub
N Seoul Tower, p011
Sulwhasoo Spa, p030
Olympic Park, pp064-065

Christopher Sturman
Leeum, Samsung Museum
of Art, pp028-029

Yang Taeu
Zagamachi, p047

Patrick Voigt
Paju Book City, p103

JH Yoon
Jeju Museum of Art, p099

SEOUL
A COLOUR-CODED GUIDE TO THE HOT 'HOODS

MYEONG-DONG
Seoul's financial district and commercial core comprises a mix of architectural styles

APGUJEONG-DONG
The capital's glitterati reign in these buzzing backstreets full of neon-lit concept shops

SEONGDONG-GU
Former warehouses have become enticing stores and cafés in an understatedly cool 'hood

SAMCHEONG-DONG
Upmarket bars and sleek eateries are springing up fast in this leafy residential enclave

HONGDAE
Away from the centre, Hongdae is a youthful, high-energy hub of creativity and culture

ITAEWON-DONG
Sophisticated coffee stops and clubs now dot a neighbourhood once filled with expats

CHEONGDAM-DONG
This high-end retail heartland is the place to come for your designer labels and latte fix

SINSA-DONG
Happening restaurants and lounges abound here and attract a fashion-forward crowd

For a full description of each neighbourhood, see the Introduction.
Featured venues are colour-coded, according to the district in which they are located.